RED STUDIO

RED STUDIO

MARY CORNISH

Oberlin College Press
Oberlin, Ohio

The FIELD Poetry Series, Volume 20
Oberlin College Press, 50 N. Professor St., Oberlin, OH 44074
www.oberlin.edu/ocpress

Cover painting: Adriaen Coorte (Dutch, ca. 1660-after 1707), *Gooseberries on a Table*, 1701. Oil on paper mounted on wood; 29.7 x 22.8 cm. © The Cleveland Museum of Art, Leonard C. Hanna, Jr., Fund 1987.32.
Cover and book design: Steve Farkas

Library of Congress Cataloging-in-Publication Data

Cornish, Mary, 1948-
  Red studio / Mary Cornish.
    p. cm. — (Field poetry series ; v. 20)
ISBN-13: 978-0-932440-31-0 (alk. paper)
ISBN-10: 0-932440-31-2 (alk. paper)
I. Title
PS3603.O768R43 2007
811'.6—dc22
                                2006101996

For Tom

CONTENTS

Part One

Restoration   1
The Laws of Japanese Painting   3
The Lane   4
Lotus Feet   5
Cut Flowers   7
Tomb Painting   8
Body Ornament   9
Tomb Ritual: The Opening of the Mouth   11
We're in the kitchen   12
Eating the Blossom   13
The Hat by Keats   14
Four Canopic Jars   15
Harp in the Form of a Woman Seated   16

Part Two

Tomb Painting: The Chapter of Breathing Air   19
One of the Shapes   20
Some Years the Berries   21
Aubade   22
Conversations with Death   23
Prelude   24
The Art of Misdirection   25
Audubon Clock   26
Woodwinds   27
That Winter   28
The angel of silence is flying over us   29
Dragonflies   30
Coffin Text   31
In the middle of the night   32

Carnal Prayer Mat   33
Beauty as an Evolutionary Strategy   35
Household Alchemy   36

Part Three

Remains   39
Fifteen Moving Parts   40
Reliquaries   43
Sideshow   44
Uncertainty Principle   46
A Long-Held Theory   47
Aerial View   48
Love and the Eiffel Tower   49
Numbers   50
Kamakura Buddha   52
We run home movies backward   53
Hand Shadows   54
Saigon Water-Puppet Show   55
Clearing the Table to Write   56
Incarnate   57
Gravity   58
Revision   59
Color Wheel   60
Hinged Earth   61
Legato   62

Notes and Acknowledgments   63

I use small brushes and never more than twelve colors.

—*Matisse*

Part One

Restoration

Everyone knew the water would rise,
but nobody knew how much.
The priest at Santa Croce said, "God
will not flood the church."
When the Arno broke its banks,
God entered as a river, left His mark high
above the altar.
He left nothing untouched:
stones, plaster, wood.
You are all my children.
The hem of His garment, which was
the river bottom's sludge,
swept through Florence, filling cars and cradles,
the eyes of marble statues,
even the Doors of Paradise. And the likeness
of the Son's hands, those pierced palms soaked
with water, began to peel like skin.
The Holy Ghost appeared
as clouds of salted crystals
on the faces of saints, until the intonaco
of their painted bodies stood out from the wall as if
they had been resurrected.

This is what I know of restoration:
in a small room near San Marco,
alone on a wooden stool
nearly every day for a year,
I painted squares of blue on gessoed boards—
cobalt blue with madder rose, viridian,
lamp black—pure pigments and the strained yolk
of an egg, then pencilled notes about the powders,
the percentages of each. I never asked

to what end I was doing what I did, and now
I'll never know. Perhaps there was one square
that matched the mantle of a penitent, the stiff
hair of a donkey's tail, a river calm beneath a bridge.
I don't even know what I learned,
except the possibilities of blue, and how God enters.

The Laws of Japanese Painting

The flower builds from the center,
each stroke in order.

The artist always kneels.

Brushes are the hair of fox,
rabbit, badger, deer.
A stroke has the strength of a cliff
when painting the cliff.

If a mountain is ten feet high, the trees
should be one foot, the horse one inch, and a man
the size of a bean.

A flower is never painted out of season.
New Year's Day: rising sun,
the pine at the gate.
Later, cock and hen with budding plum branch.

Cocks crow, *kokka koo:* happiness to our land.
Objects have no shadow.

The folds of a garment may be painted
eighteen ways, according to the eighteen laws.

The nude is never painted.

Asked to paint crows flying across four sliding doors,
the artist painted a crow's wing
disappearing from the fourth.

The Lane

Left alone with his dead body,
I took off my husband's socks,
put my face on his feet.
Unbuttoned his shirt, pulled down
his pants, stroked and kissed the legs, chest,
penis. There was nothing I did not want
to hold, although in death his body
had let go, the way I'd heard it did
if a man were hanged. There was nothing
that did not smell human.
That night, his eyes were taken, and his skin
removed for other bodies.

As I walk to town, my mind
goes back to his shape—in our bed,
on that stainless table.
Crossing the bridge, I think of a scene
that Constable painted over and over: the lane
from his native village to the one
where his father owned a mill. Blue
cart tracks set against the warm-toned
road. Near hills, a touch of orange.
He'd go back there with his brush, lay down
those small, deliberate strokes, again and again.

Lotus Feet

The desire to be bound came as a man comes,
falling against a breast,
the way a silken helplessness arrives, ripe
as a plum. To keep him near, I made of my feet
twin bamboo shoots,
three inches long, pale as moons.

I washed and rubbed each foot with alum,
pulling four toes to the arch, binding them
toward the heel, wrapping the cut cloth tighter—
over and under my instep: right foot, left—
until the bones burned in grief.

At each rebinding, I bled; flesh fell away:
my feet became slender as willow twigs,
smaller than my hands.

      *

When I walk, each muted step calls out his name.
I no longer work in the fields.
Two doves of silent prayer, my feet have transcended earth.
They're lofty as verse: *fox fairies, winter cherries,*
dragons playing with a pearl. At night, they wake with fire.

      *

This is my masquerade: golden lotuses
under a green skirt, keeping my secret.
Although a powdered fragrance fills my shoes,
the odor of decay seeps through.
In this way, I join him.

*

Only he could touch my feet, hold them to his cheek.
All night, I wore my slippers in bed;
we played *Twofold Joy* and *Lovebird on One Foot.*

*

My needle has inscribed a line of text
on each embroidered cuff:

Light rain: the grass a kind of bride,
breathless against the earth.

The scene below the cuff is motionless,
a tiny garden of stitches: flowers, clouds;
no breeze moves the leaves.
In this way, I am steadfast.
If I could lift my feet around his waist—
again, two swallows, flying.

Beside a tray of dumplings, water chestnuts, fish,
we slept. Now, I dream of snow: my feet are hooks,
the delicate hooves of deer.

Cut Flowers

Because I want the blooms to last,
I scald the stems
of roses, hold an orange poppy to a match
until the milk burns in the flame.
It's an art they call *conditioning*.
I crush the base of a chrysanthemum—
the heads keep blooming, rootless,
like the flower heads that float
on Chinese screens.

I add sugar to the vase, a tablespoon
to ease the shock.
Who knows how a cut stem enters water?
Seen through glass, this green stalk
seems to shift as it hits
the line between one element
and the next: it's a trick of light, sometimes
I'll walk into a windowed room
and can't remember why.

Tomb Painting

The boat of the earth is a tunnel,
a bull's head at either end.
We pass through the skin of the bull.
In this scene, the wife holds grain;
the writing says, *May the bread fly up,*
may the bread continue to fly up to my house.

Offshore, the boat, the man's body
like another sun going down, east to west.
It glides through a door in the Field of Reeds,
the bolt of the horizon slides:
a face falls on a face.

The oars have eyes, they foresee arrival,
riverbanks flooding with mud—beetle-god,
crocodile-god, frog-headed god.
They come who have torn a piece of it.
Open-winged, birds keel, as though they flew
through more than the memory of air.

On a boat with no mast, judgment drifts,
an ape beats a pig. Red ink, black ink:
a heart is weighed.

The wife is not dead, yet she rides the Night Barge,
chair behind her husband's chair,
as if they still slept back-to-belly in their bed—
that fit of curves and hollows we call *sleeping spoons*—
the silvery way they moved, like fish,
below the water of their sleep.

Body Ornament

Henna

From a leafy curtain, the parrots
spoke with a human voice;
they seemed like small, green gods.
You could hear me then.

Across my palms, I drew
three waves the color of earth,
like the mouth of a river.

I painted my fingers with eyes—
you could see me then.

To please you, I painted my nipples with stars
so night would fall. The gods were incidental.

Before daylight, they approached
as through a field of rushes.
Your mouth filled with silt.

River and *throne* were errors in translation,
the dead rising from the heads of lilies.

*

Piercing

I pierced my lip with silver.
I pierced my tongue. It was mute.
I pierced the flesh above my eye.
Where are you if not in the wound?

*

Tattoo

All night, ink blooms
while I sleep. The needle sings.
It's making a garden under my skin.

On either thigh, a peony, its heavy head
like yours between my legs.

A flush of pink along the petals,
my body aroused—

for years, I knew you like this.

Stems greening my calves. On my arms, the vines.
Their underside in shade, the roots awake.

New moon: the eye of the sky is closed.
You sit in a blue chair under a tree.
In the garden, you return.

Full moon: a gold carp swimming up my back,
another down. They ripple as I move above you.

Their eyes alive.

All night, the needle stings,
each inch of me in leaf, and you return.

On my breasts, the birds, the flight.

Tomb Ritual: The Opening of the Mouth

With the metal blade of an adze,
I split your closed mouth open—
with the foreleg of an ox,
*   the knife of heaven,*
*   the fingers of one hand:*

Four times awakened.

We're in the kitchen

on a summer's afternoon. I wear
that dress you've always liked, the one
without a zipper, any buttons, just
held up by the patterned flight of birds
along the cotton. I'm washing grapes.
You're reading travel magazines out loud.
"Visitors," you read, "can hear the deep Aegean Sea
in silver shells called Aphrodite's ears."

As if we'd crossed that sea of Kodak blue
and disembarked along the island's shore,
we follow the narrative of whitewashed houses
clinging to a cliff. A woman at a bus stop
puts on lipstick. Outside a tavern door, five men
sit drinking wine and playing cards.
One holds his hand, like a sorrow, close
to his chest, while ash-green trees
are making olives out of wind and stone.
Later, when the sun beats
on white tablecloths, the day
is dizzy with the smell of female goats.

Inside the town museum, under glass, two bees
are clasped in gold, forever
sucking on a single bead of honey.
Near the exit stairs, a goddess
lifts her bare breasts, holds
a snake in either hand, and smiles as though
she were a woman passing by.
Waves move against the seawall,
rocking small boats, light
as flags. You come up behind me, slip
both hands beneath my dress.
Even the birds are reeling.

Eating the Blossom

The petals in his mouth, that scent
like ruins, and the island opening
in his mind: no wind, no stars—
the lotus-eater forgot a wife, a sea,
the boat as it floated off.
He even forgot to grieve.

Who wants the hour to be always noon,
to nap without long shadows?

Each morning, the wife at her loom
reassembles air and bird, then
smaller still, the leaves.
She weaves the gods: one high,
another by a river, resting.
Her shuttle gives the illusion
of movement, its gesture forward,
the insistence on return.

In another room, someone is speaking.
Beyond her hands, entreaties.

Each night, she cuts the thread: herons
lift, and cliffs fall under the blade.
She presses her mouth against a woven blossom
as if it were a husband, his absence on her tongue
unsaying *sun hill tree,* her fingers undoing
the gods—their threadless eyes
above white stones, the shore
a different shore:

Did you think I wouldn't find you?

All night alone, she unmakes the house, the roof.

The Hat by Keats

I do believe if I could be a hatter I might be one.
—John Keats

Each day the snakes
shift shape beneath a veil.
Each day the roses spill
through fronds of tulle.

A length of watered silk
surrounds the crown and briefly
laps green leaves: inconstant,
any shore where land ends.

Its firmament of straw achieves
a weightlessness, yet smells of fields
cut early, draws us to the earth
like horses grazing.

A goldfinch, glass eye fixed
and shining, clings
to the down-turned brim
like joy to a man's heart.

Can you see how the bird loved thistles—
loved even the shadows of thistles?

Four Canopic Jars

Among the earthen crocks of wine and grain,
four jars store human viscera.
Flank of the body cut open, entrails removed,
cavity cleansed, anointed,
anus injected with oil.

The stoppers of the jars are gods:
a man-head guards the liver;
a jackal guards the stomach;
a falcon broods over guts;
a baboon squats on the lungs.

Harp in the Form of a Woman Seated

Three strings tighten
at her throat: the rounded pegs,
their turning.

Gulls circle, ash on their wings.
Circle of sea, ash falling.

Across her breast, the hide
skinned clean, then dried.
A small hole cut for speaking.

Salt in the waves, salt
in the wound.

From barren fields,
the black seeds of her eyes,
the ox-bone teeth.

Men quarrel from coffins.
The rinsed stones of their fists.

Her hair a lamentation
of chaff, the wind
as evidence.

From thigh to thigh
across my lap,
the tide is coming in.

Part Two

Tomb Painting: The Chapter of Breathing Air

The king's soul as a bird,
hawk-wings spread, hovers
above the coffin-face: they almost kiss.

Beware of thy border, which is in Earth.

Still, the river flows north, the land depicted
is the same black silt—abundant.
Oh desert, thou art washed.

Are the man and woman eating honeyed cakes
in this world or the next?

No man becomes a star without a companion.

Shall I be thy companion?

Once more, the pintail ducks are flying
over the bricklayer's house.
Spools are filled with twine.
Loaves cool on a plank,
and the milk jug's carried home in a net.
On a roof where they slept in the open air,
hairpins in the same clay bowl.

One of the Shapes

These figs: meaning Eden over and over.
A paperwhite narcissus by the bed.
We lie on damp sheets, windows open to a garden
where the quince blooms a fever of blooms, bares
its desire like breasts. The women who blackened
their teeth for beauty were not unlike the quince—
they gilded their lower lips, rouged the tips
of their tongues.

That shape, veiled, unveiled.
Skunk cabbage lifting its hooded spathe along
the water's edge: a foetid stink. And the rank smell
of a bitch fox on warm air. Tonight we'll hear her
yelping to be mated, a need sharp as those barks.
If I wash at my mirror, the shadow cast is vixen-like:
its movement disturbs the room. All March, her calling.

Some Years the Berries

This year the berries are plentiful.
They cluster on pokeweed and wild cohosh
under the bridge. Even the elms in town
are seldom bare: bluejays crown the branches.
We sit by the window in a red vinyl booth,
winter coats and mufflers on the bench,
and drink mint tea from paper cups.
The waitress says she's going home to Egypt—
she has a Nefertiti nose. We talk of sun
and sugared dates along the Nile.
And when you search your pockets for the tip,
spilling change into my open palms, the gold fan
of a ginko leaf falls out among the coins.

Aubade

You're still asleep in the night before,
and I'm awake in a different day:
vine maples, upright on the sky,
rest upside-down across the lake below.
How silent our house
the morning after a party.

On the table, gobs of cake, a wine-
stained cloth, grapes
rolled beneath a plate.
I move from dining room
to kitchen sink and back—
restoring order, suspended in the hour.
A red geranium drops petals
on the floor. Sofa cushions hold
the shape of friends.

I right a wooden chair that tilts
against the wall like those
of Shanghai acrobats: the skill
in resting one chair on four glasses
on a painted table, then an added chair,
then three, then four, and at the top
of that pagoda,
a woman balanced on one hand.

Conversations with Death

Often, you don't speak at all,
the surfaces of days are cool as mirrors.

Then, your face stitched to a linen shroud
sees me brushing my hair, says *Look at my curls*.

Once a woman rode my husband like a bull. Still
I feel the whip of her breasts, his need for ruin.

Stone bird, you sharpen your beak,
one claw in me, the other on a wheel that rolls—

My children reached the wall of the world
and couldn't enter. Always, their songs are cradles.

Your voice says *Look at my lips*.

Prelude

"I would term the Preludes strange. They are sketches,
beginnings of études, or, so to speak, ruins…"
        —*Robert Schumann*

This is Chopin's secret: an orange is orange
because a night chill enters the skin
like a theme.

        Peeled, each globe suggests
a planet's longitudes, imaginary bands
that mark the measures. There's a depth of field
to the sphinx moth, as G-sharp emerges
in the sirocco's dust-wind lifting across the Sahara,
growing heavy and damp toward Palma,
gusting in the harbor outside his window:
At night for long hours, I hear songs…

        Suppose a lizard's quick eye
watched us stroll one golden section
of the earth's geography—cedars,
figs, sun over Mallorca—
and nothing bound to happen next.

The Art of Misdirection

The pledge, that language with the wingspan of a canary,
flutters from the conjuror's hand, startled by footlights,
feathers bright as blown glass, as if—before this point of entry—
it had been sitting in a lemon tree.

Messieurs, Mesdames, there's nothing up his sleeve.

Now *the turn*, as the assistant gestures toward reversal.
She might as well be undoing the third day,
those laws of earth and sea, the way her body overflows
her bustier. You're thinking *lip* and *shore*, you're thinking *bed
of roses*—while the bird, wings beating, slips through a pinhole
in the firmament. Such is the hocus pocus
of a solid world turning through thin air.

Later, a silk scarf pulled from your pocket
like The Theory of a Unified Field, opens.
The canary flies from its folds, small trumpet of deliverance.
You're glad to have it back, although the vanishing
has made it sing the liquid song of bees.
This is *the prestige,* the breathe-life-into, as when

a woman sawed in half stands up whole
and lifts her arms, her leotard a skin of gold coins.
Each time before the lights come up,
she lies in the limbo of the turn, saw descending,
red box with its glitter-stars wheeling her in two
until her feet are seen at a great distance from her head—

her torso interrupted,
and the illusionist walking through that space,
his smoky promise, his mirrored hall.

Audubon Clock

Every hour on the hour, a new bird
flies through the house.
This morning, the throat
of a small brown wren
opened the beak of day. I heard
its high scale fall.

At eight, a sparrow called, *kettle,*
kettle, kettle...
above the mild confusion of the rooms:
stockings in the sink, floor unswept.
And a mockingbird mocked
the ups and downs of household tales:
walls of sugar, eggs of gold,
and the one where—in broad daylight—
the cook fell asleep by the pot,
the dogs in the yard,
even the fire slept.

Tonight, I'll lie in bed, listen
for the horned owl's low
hoo-hooo... once, then again.
I'll remember an owl that hunted
from the peak of another house,
in its abandoned roost,
the coughed-up hair,
the small, clean bones.

Woodwinds

It's only air, but blown
across a bottle's lip, it moves a boat
through fog.
                    In low mist
over the Ganges, corpses drift
among the floating heads of marigolds.
Onshore, a flute's alive with wind,
the cobra's ribs are sails.

                    *

I once blew lightly into a frog's mouth
through a Dixie straw—the frog
pinned to a board—the lesson:
how lungs lift and fall.
                                        A whale
breaks the surface of the sea
to catch its breath from a blowhole's
single nostril. Even a slug—
the least of my brethren—
crossing the field on a ribbon of mucus,
has something like a lung.

                    *

All summer, wind
in trees outside our window:
bird-note, leaf-fall, the neighbor calling
her lost dog—
                    my own breath
whistling through a blade of grass
between two thumbs,
as if I were an instrument of air.

That Winter

That winter, we pulled down the nest
      the martins had abandoned early:
a mess of sodden straw, dung.
      Inside the box, small bodies graying—two dead young.

The vines we pruned late
      bled their sap onto the snow all March.
We waited for warm weather.
      When we slept, our sleep was flightless, feathered.

April—vines sent out green flags.
      The sap sealed over. Still, leaves frosted
where stems dragged the ground. You called
      for me to see the greening and the scars. Snowfall

reached the dog's belly.
      Sticks we'd broken last year marked
where spotted lilies came up in the woods.
      You tied back vines, I held the twine between us. It was good.

The angel of silence is flying over us

—*Chekhov*

How little it takes to suggest a garden:
a chestnut leaf on a wooden bench,
stage left. Elsewhere—beyond the lake
with its heavy-lidded toads,
beyond the flowerbeds of windless days, fetid iris,
horses hauling rye—
the tree shades fields whose furrows vanish
in a point of sun.

Light shines on Masha in black silk:
"I am," she says,
"in mourning for my life."
Then hours of speech disguise
each gesture's mute plea:
                    (grabs his arm),
                    (clutches her breast),
                    (waltzes alone for two or three turns)…
Summer's light encircles Masha,
her outstretched hand a chestnut leaf:
five veined fingers and a palm turned up.

Dragonflies

Every age is an age of flying dragons:
they wrap their tails around the earth,
they're ridden by the Dead
who watch us wake.
Between two worlds, they rest
on blades of grass, their bodies scarcely bend
the tips. Even their days are weightless.

At the pond's edge, tiger beetles
breed, toads and salamanders spawn.
Vesper Bluets, winged like grace notes,
sweep the quiet surface. Citrine
Forktails, Spangled Skimmers skim.

Born as naiads, they travel
wordless: wandering the rivers
of Hades, crossing thresholds,
stepping from their skeletons to be
the devil's needles.
We can barely hear their dry rasp over water
when—simple as *Come home*—
they sew our eyelids shut.

Coffin Text

Lihir al Imar

Badussa numina, numina al laman
in duhir minabab.
"Pidu, pidu," rumana al tira bidin.
Lodina him bab al amir ina malara dumassan.
Den loma ma suba—
Wulora padem medora!
Im bruma mahin wituba.
Im dom al adib.
Badussa numina, numina al laman
in duhir minabab.

Waiting by the Nile

I sit at night, at night by the hull
of the overturned boat.
Pidu, pidu, call the shorebirds.
Small silver fish skip like stones on the water.
Later, I will drop my net—
Delicious breakfast of *padem* fish!
Far off the thorns of desert scrub.
Far off the horns of the viper.
I sit at night, at night by the hull
of the overturned boat.

In the middle of the night

in the bed beneath my bed,
a woman weeps. I turn
the television down to hear her
through the floor.
In the kitchen beneath my kitchen,
she dumps the knives and forks and spoons
out of a drawer and cleans
each corner of the plastic tray.

Now I stand reflected
by a full-length mirror
on the bathroom door. She's there
in her nightgown, only
a floor below.
Because I cannot think
of anything else to give, I open
both taps in the tub and let the water run
to make a sound that carries.

Carnal Prayer Mat

I'm crossing a bridge
to the Lantern Festival
in a poem by Li Ch'ing-chao.

My lips are red,
my jacket gold-threaded,
my hair-ornament winged.

All night, paired dragonflies dart
between the large-leafed mulberries.
Grief cannot find me.

      *

I'm entering a still-life by Bonnard, off-center
in a doorway to the left. The room is not yet
quite awake, and so its walls are slanted;
stripes of sun fall through a painted floor.
The dog, as marginal as I am, sniffs
a busy tablecloth where checks of red and white
collide with chairs: a blue vase
skitters, flowers riot, even the sugar bowl
tilts toward an open balcony. Cicadas
must be buzzing their crooked summer songs.

      *

I'm lying in the high grass
of a Mozart flute quartet.

How tired I am of everything I know!

Slowly, Latin names begin to lift
off tree limbs, off the backs of bugs.
Even my own three names rise up
and disappear over a hill.

Beauty as an Evolutionary Strategy

For example, this poppy, its petals sudden as blood.
In a garden of grays, the bee sees red as black,
dusts the darkest flower. And in technicolor,
James Dean, the strategy of t-shirts, Lucky Strikes
rolled in one sleeve. That high-voltage
restlessness. Shy girls, bewildered boys,
drawn to the curve of his arms on film,
a tactic of tissue and pulse.

The beauty of Titian's Peter—you'd swear
those painted arms were flesh.
He's fishing with Andrew, the two of them arguing,
hauling their heavy nets into the boat.
They bend to the lake's mirror: among reflected reeds,
a heron's image turning its liquid head to hunt.
And the floating shapes of men—necks, lips, bellies—
their bodies' second life on the surface of water.

Household Alchemy

Five pears in a wooden bowl,
sun on the table—cause enough
for celebration or defeat: the skin
of fruit, the flesh of trees.
Out of such ripening, the self
could step from the bowl of the world
into light on pears—
                      as when children
play Hide the Thimble: the object
always hidden in plain sight,
the search that turns a solid house
quicksilver. Rain falls on the glass
in every room; a curtain flickers
over the sink; the sill moves
in and out of shadow.
And the children say,
You're getting cold,
you're getting very hot.
                    Now, leaves fuse
on the window, shimmer
from a moving branch outside.
Light breathes on the table
across my husband's hand—
                    It is smoke
and a cloud, and fugitive servant...

The flame of five pears, gold
as honey, the stillness of the bowl
that holds them in plain sight.
In the wheel-fire of the world:
We're getting hot. We're burning.

Part Three

Remains

The baker's body was found, spiced
with cloves and wrapped
in the lost lyrics of Sappho.
For years, he lay in the sand, her song
against his cheek: *thin fire*
runs like a thief through my body.

A single feather drifts
out of the sky, but the rook flies on.

Not broken, not beyond repair,
but gone—the whole
that leaves behind a part, a city
humbled to its artifacts:
plate, doll, ring.

A tube of lipstick,
fallen from a boat,
rusts at the bottom of a lake—
even daylight crumbles
into sleep: its fragments bob and nod
to one another as they pass.

And figments of the night
linger during breakfast,
where the scent of China tea still clings
inside an empty pot.

Fifteen Moving Parts

Unearthed in a Chinese village
a miniature box on wheels
designed in bronze
with fifteen moving parts:
six turning wheels,
four hinged openings,
a sliding door bolt,
four pivoting birds,
two coiled snakes,
and human guards,
including the one-legged doorkeeper
who might have been chosen
simply because
he could not easily run off.

*

In a Chinese village or any village where fog rolls in when you had hoped
to see the outline of trees, some part of the scroll is always missing:

        ] beside the doorsill [
           ] and she with her arm out as if to [
            ] like [   ] with her basket.

*

A miniature box on wheels is a perfect hiding place for letters from a lover,
powdered seashells used to whiten skin. Each subject has a nature: fish-
hook, storm, desire.

*

Designed in bronze, it may have been a child's toy. Every autumn, the one-legged doorkeeper's children played leap-frog under a pear tree.

*

Fifteen moving parts are not a lot compared to the parts of a body that move, compared to the movements of stars, compared to those things that move which we would like to stand still. In rain, the bamboo leaves hang down; in wind they cross, confused.

*

Six turning wheels are traveling over potholes now, or along the edge of a sea. The empire of the wind moves through trees, but the travelers can't hear its *sha sha sha* over the noise of wheels.

*

Four hinged openings let in light, which enters differently from light in a field, the way a beam catches particles of dust, looks like a holy presence, is condensed in shafts that pierce the box.

*

A sliding door bolt puts our minds at ease. Yet at any time, the lover might write: "The sumac shows traces of red. Go home, go home."

*

Four pivoting birds could see the story whole, perched as they are, on four corners; but they are distracted by the sight of a cornfield over the next hill.

*

Two coiled snakes form a universe of motion. To put the dot in a viper's eye, the artist dwelt for years in the dot. Here, lidless eyes are open.

*

And human guards are not distinguishable from human thieves as far as snakes are concerned, or saints from sinners,

*

including the one-legged doorkeeper, with his missing leg, like the missing part of the story, the part that explains

*

who might have been chosen. But who isn't chosen

*

simply because a bird flies through an open field? And the wheels are turning, and the door bolt sliding, with the finger of providence doling out blessings and curses—which of these he'd been given the doorkeeper couldn't quite know. But his wife and his children and small house and dog (all undepicted) would greet his arrival and take off his boot and sit with him out in the garden from which

*

he could not easily run off.

Reliquaries

This is where they keep the bits and pieces
of saints, in silver-gilded boxes
walled with beveled glass
to pretend that God's house is transparent.

Here's a hair from St. Cecilia's head, cut
like thread for the needle's eye, that unblinking gate
to heaven. Here's skin from the wound
of a saint who preached to birds
in a dream of tongues—
as if winged creatures needed teaching,
loved, as they are, by angels.

This is the mystery I adore: the odd
finger. The belovèd tooth. The blood-
soaked cheek of Saint Catherine
after the wheel. Even a scrap of the robe
Judas wore as he walked the rose-scented earth
on two bare feet with Christ, and leaned
into the kiss. The sky is so far away,
and the body's such a strange home.

Sideshow

Let those who are in favor with their stars
see order in the shapes of constellations:
ram and fish and bull. Other men are born
on nights when random stars make variations
of the human: giants, dwarfs, two-headed
freaks. The sideshow lobster boy descended
from a family of cleft hands, followed
carnivals until his story ended.
Who hears the noise of ocean creatures seep
into our dreams? Starfish voices, eels that wail
beneath the surface. What force could ever keep
the crying out? When Lobster Boy was grown,
his son's and daughter's hands were cleft as well.
He drank, he beat his wife. She had him killed.

*

The Tocci brothers had four arms, two heads,
but joined from the sixth rib down, they shared
one-half a torso, anus, and two legs.
Confronted by this freak, the Church declared
that they were two (not one two-headed man),
and so they had two souls to go to hell
or heaven, and the exercise of will,
as free as any God-made man can have.
Three buttocks sat and one blood flowed
around the liver and the gut into
two brains. And when the single penis rose,
whose hand drove whose desire to its peak?
On stage they dressed in velvet suit, fine laces.
At home, undressed one body with two faces.

*

Dreamland was the only show with geeks
beside the sea. Here, Samuel Gumpertz built
a half-scale Nuremberg for half-sized freaks
to take up residence year-round. The little
Lilliputia had fire trucks, false alarms
that sounded once an hour. When city lights
went down, the midgets fell asleep in charming
midget beds like Snow White's seven dwarfs.
A girl who ate the heads off chickens slept
along Surf Avenue with dog-faced boys
and lizard men, while Zip the pinhead kept
a moron's watch on Coney Island Pier.
All night, the freaks would sleep, the tide would rise—
they'd drift without their hands, their legs, their eyes.

Uncertainty Principle

Things hold their secrets, Heraclitus said. This field,
the logic of thistles. And in grass,
whatever's horned or spiked, surviving.

Above the litany of thorns, the curve
of a California hill, the roundness of oaks.
Even Time, which never was an arrow,
curves where it meets an object.

The moth's wing mimics a great eye,
on the recluse spider's head, a violin—
form as destiny or riddle:
I've one mouth but many voices;
I dissemble, and often change my tune...

Now, somewhere closer to the oaks, a kingbird
perches like a second hand before the hour:
this one field, and various secrets—
moth, thistle, bell.

A Long-Held Theory

Eager to prove both egg and semen
vital to the mystery
of generation, 18th century ovist
Lazzaro Spallanzani sewed
waxed taffeta trousers for a frog
who rubbed and rubbed against a female
of the species, never skin
to skin, the egg never
quickening for want
of having been *bedewed*,
by droplets of the male found
in his pants—
                        a test designed
with such simplicity to prove
a long-held theory science
labels *elegant*, a word I'd use
for figures on a Greek vase:
him chasing her, his left foot forward,
calves exposed, a spear
in his right hand and in his left
her wrist; her looking over her shoulder
as she flees, her gown in folds
between her thighs and his,
her right heel off the ground
for centuries.

Aerial View

I watch the fiction of the round globe
settle into its old, flat map, the ocean's foam
no more than Spanish lace through which
ships sailed to the known world's edge.

The woman in the aisle seat's asleep
inside her body's journey: one hand folded
on another, woolen skirt in drapes along her knee,
even her tissued eyelids creased.
I'm thinking of the contours of the female sex
beneath her clothes and mine, how we hold
our pleated lives—like paper fans—
one side turned out, the other turned away.

Love and the Eiffel Tower

In love with fame, or speed,
or the invention of the wheel,
the mayor of Montmartre rode
his bicycle down the Eiffel Tower
and lived. A tailor at the turn
of the century sewed a cape
to fly from one of the iron decks: he broke
his neck, but first, the heart
exploded in his chest. Did he love
the plunge of his body's needle
through the flat silk of the sky?
And then there was the man
in love with Death, who jumped
and landed on a car; he married
the driver.
         Those who think
love travels far, lands safe,
tie notes to the tails
of balloons and float them off
the rails. One message rose to drift
over the Museum of Mankind, look down
at men and women, at the Seine,
its quiet water. Then,
free of riverbanks, the rules
of source and sea, was smitten by a breeze.
Transported easily, the single note
swept through the laws of probability,
across the Pyrenees, over
Hungarian cows—past sun,
through clouds of rain, and settled
in a potato field.

Numbers

I like the generosity of numbers.
The way, for example,
they are willing to count
anything or anyone:
two pickles, one door to the room,
eight dancers dressed as swans.

I like the domesticity of addition—
add two cups of milk and stir—
the sense of plenty: six plums
on the ground, three more
falling from the tree.

And multiplication's school
of fish times fish,
whose silver bodies breed
beneath the shadow
of a boat.

Even subtraction is never loss,
just addition somewhere else:
five sparrows take away two,
the two in someone else's
garden now.

There's an amplitude to long division,
as it opens Chinese take-out
box by paper box,
inside every folded cookie
a new fortune.

And I never fail to be surprised
by the gift of an odd remainder,
footloose at the end:
forty-seven divided by eleven equals four,
with three remaining.
Three boys beyond their mothers' call,
two Italians off to the sea,
one sock that isn't anywhere you look.

Kamakura Buddha

On a day made for strolling, I follow the curve
into a courtyard where the giant Buddha sits.
Birds flutter, fly up in his face:
the hands rest on the folded legs.
There is no effort to his weight.
One day, he found this garden
and sat down—on an afternoon made for sitting—
after the cherry blossoms fell, and the azaleas
were unfolding their simple stars.
Even then, his body was slowly turning
green, and the children
ran in circles, chasing pigeons.

We run home movies backward

just to see your waving hand become
a fluttering retreat, its odd good-bye
sucked down to the pool where you and I
are vaulted in a flip of anti-gravity, plucked
from the water like two pink shrimp,
our double splash snatched back
into the blue abyss, the water
closing over our disappearance
while we complete the arc's descent,
landing without impact on the pink tiles—
then the squeal before our plunge,
the nudge, the pose we strike.
We're walking backward in that jerky way
toward the double sliding doors,

and if death is Bergman's reaper,
then the joke's on him. Turtle and giraffe
around our waists, we're moving frame by frame
toward the morning of that California day,
away from subtitles, Sweden's cold.

Hand Shadows

My father put his hands in the white light
of the lantern, and his palms became a horse
that flicked its ears and bucked; an alligator
feigning sleep along the canvas wall leapt up
and snapped its jaws in silhouette, or else
a swan would turn its perfect neck and drop
a fingered beak toward that shadowed head
to lightly preen my father's feathered hair.
Outside our tent, skunks shuffled in the woods
beneath a star that died a little every day,
and from a nebula of light diffused
inside Orion's sword, new stars were born.
My father's hands became two birds, linked
by a thumb, they flew one following the other.

Saigon Water-Puppet Show

The husband throws his fish net
in a lake, the wife draws it back,
full of fish.
Buffaloes move slowly
on underwater wires
and the music of a single voice
trembles through the grass.

A fox sneaks into the flock
of an old peasant couple; they worry
about their ducks. The singer quacks, *cap*
cap, and children laugh. Everyone
helps save the smallest duck.
Later, two gold phoenix rise,
male and female, from the water.

Under a full moon, lions fight
to possess a colored ball.
Then, peace comes. Wooden dragons dance
in lakes and ponds while villagers admire
their wild, celestial swim.
The dragon-puppets breathe real fire, dip
beneath the pool and spout
real water at the crowd that cheers.

Puppeteers come out
from behind the bamboo curtain,
dragons in their arms—
we all applaud. A man in hip-boots says
it took him all his life
to learn the Dance of the Immortals.
He says this, then he bows.

Clearing the Table to Write

—Or else the Chinese bowl comes first,
plain white where it is meant to hold food,
and where my hands are meant to hold the bowl,
a scene in ultramarine: willow trees and duckweed,
the usual river between cliffs, cooking smoke
that rises from a small boat—all in that shade
once mixed from copper and blood.
Like an apparition, or a blueprint.

Incarnate

Again, the warrior died. His body was rinsed with seawater,
a coin placed in the mouth for travel, his chin strapped with linen
to keep the jaws from opening.

The funeral fire was a tight bud that flared
to full bloom, and when his corpse burst back to life,
even the orbs of his eyes were burning.
Beside him, a donkey rolled its head, the pig
was a window of ash. The lizard flamed out like a twig.

As if they were strangers arriving at the gates of a city,
an arch defined the proscenium.
The traveler was lost, or he was not—
omnia mutantur: all is transfigured.

Orpheus took the shape of a swan,
each cob and pen mated for life,
his fate no longer mythic, just a nest over the muskrat's den.

On the sarcophagus, mourners lift their hands as if to tear their hair,
but in tomb-light, it looks like they're waving.

Odysseus wished to be ordinary:
in this revival of the story, a man pumps gas
while his wife pours coffee from a thermos, passes the lid.
The radio plays *La Vie en Rose*.
(Somewhere it's noon, a four-legged wind is watching.)

If a midwife marks the newborn's face with spit,
quick-fingered, a soul sits down in the body.
The urge to flesh is skeletal and sly:
Ajax chose a lion's teeth, Agamemnon, an eagle's claws—
even now, someone's hatching into feather and beak.

Gravity

Bread's rising, spreading its yeasty smell
even to the backyard where Italian plums
have ripened early. Once, in Umbria,
I saw persimmons fall on terraced hills,
their rotting skins medieval, like a tapestry.
No fruit stays on the branch—we know the law
of falling bodies binding us to earth, and so
we want to make things rise. Kites lift, planes fly,
a cow jumps over a waning moon.
We build a dome the experts say won't hold,
paint false stars golden, the vault sky blue
over the bones of Assisi's patron saint.
The fact that Giotto's nave has fallen
doesn't mean it wasn't really heaven.

Revision

No wonder Watteau has turned
to wipe the red chalk from his fingers.
Gone is the *première pensée*,
the sketch that flies through the hand
like a thought through the mind.
Already there's a second set of lines
along the neck's curved nape,
an over-worked curl he's pushed
to complete understanding.

Now the girl is free to break the pose
and move around the room. She's already
forgotten what she was thinking
as she stands before the mirror with a hat.
The cat laps milk; a breeze comes
from the northeast through the window
to her upswept hair, across the cat's paws
and the artist's busy hands.

A postcard of the final drawing,
pinned above my desk, shows two poses
of the girl without a hat; two others
with the hat on, head held low.
At my back, the one true shape
of hair and cat and hand
still travels that Paris room, air
through an open window.

Color Wheel

Red clover isn't red
the way the bottom of a boat
is red, especially where it meets
a green lake.
Red clover's more like
purple, where the smooth globe
turns to meet the shadow side
of a yellow pear.
That is, the clover's head
is purple, but not actually a head,
not one that turns and looks.
Even this red clover,
false in one way or another,
has three true leaves,
which is all anybody could wish for
under a sky which is blue,
especially where it meets
an orange sun.

Hinged Earth

Although this is not a photograph, the frame
has stopped all motion. There's plenty of time
to consider the view: oak leaves, apples.
We must be in the garden, *on earth as it is.*
Hinged earth—the snake's jaw as a music box, opens
then shuts. Birds shift in flight, acorns fall;
the sky, the ground, make their small adjustments.
On earth as if at an altar: knees bend, a gill
flaps for air. The wooded canopy over it all
is thought to represent justice. Elsewhere, a dragonfly
spreads its wings on the live pin of its body—
a verb between fluttering nouns. To the left is a cliff:
there's a question of scale. You once put your hand
on the small of my back; we moved like a chord
below an ascending melody, a rare *Te Deum* in a minor key.

Legato

(Italian: bound)

As when a crow flies up from a field, the sky
accepts the weight of birds.
The crow's shadow falls to earth, and earth
accepts the shadow as if it were a house or tree.
Roots go down, blind as moles
and as eager. And in the house, each day
light moves across the bed.

Even with you gone, light moves on the bed
and I wake up. There's an arc
between the living and the dead, as when
a crow rises from a field, sun on its back.
Below, the shadow moving.

Notes and Acknowledgments

The laws of Japanese painting (in the poem of that name) were taken from various sources, including a book of that title by H. P. Bowie (1911).

Some lines in the Egyptian poems are quotations from the Pyramid of Unas texts.

"Prelude": *At night for long hours, I hear songs* is from Chopin's diary.

The first line of "Sideshow" is the first line of Shakespeare's sonnet #25.

***

I wish to thank the editors of the following journals in which some of these poems originally appeared, at times in earlier forms:

Alaska Quarterly: "We run home movies backward"
FIELD: "Cut Flowers," "Incarnation," "Hinged Earth"
New England Review: "The Laws of Japanese Painting," "Restoration," "The Lane," "Lotus Feet"
Poetry: "Numbers," "Revision"
Poetry Northwest: "Gravity," "Reliquaries"

Grateful acknowledgment is made to the Wallace E. Stegner Fellowship Program at Stanford University for its support.

I'm particularly indebted to mentors and friends at Sarah Lawrence College for their generous encouragement of my work; and to my sister and fellow poet Julie Larios for her close and tireless reading of the poems. To you—*to each of you*—my thanks.

Finally, my gratitude to David Young and David Walker for taking this collection from manuscript to book.